A WORLD OF COOKIES FOR SANTA

Follow Santa's Tasty Trip Around the World

By M.E. Furman ❄ Illustrated by Susan Gal

HOUGHTON MIFFLIN HARCOURT
Boston New York

For Bryce, who first
welcomed Santa to our house; and Kyle,
who always makes sure he gets cookies.—M.E.F

For David and Elaine, with sweet memories of cookies
and Christmases past. —S.G.

www.hmhco.com

The illustrations in this book were created with charcoal on paper and digital collage.
The text type was set in ITC Goudy Sans.
The display type was set in Mister Sirloin.

Library of Congress Cataloging-in-Publication Data is on file.
ISBN 978-0-544-22620-3

Manufactured in China
SCP 10 9 8 7 6 5 4 3 2 1
4500661215

All around the world, Christmas is a time of giving. While Santa Claus (also called Papai Noel, Father Christmas, Grandfather Frost, and more) packs his sleigh with gifts for children everywhere, they're preparing their own sweet gifts for him. Follow along on Santa's tasty trip around the globe, country by country and cookie by "cookie."

CHRISTMAS ISLAND

Kiritimati, also known as Christmas Island, is the first place in the world to welcome Christmas Day—and Santa! Children on this little island in the southern Pacific share their abundant coconut crop and leave him sweet, chewy coconut macaroons.

NEW ZEALAND

In New Zealand, children remember the reindeer, too, and leave hay or carrots for them, as well as crunchy Anzac biscuits and milk for Santa.

AUSTRALIA

Santa Claus uses his magic key to open the front door when he visits children in Australia. He leaves small gifts in a sack or stocking by their bedrooms, and their bigger gifts under the tree.

Their gift to him is crispy, fruit-filled "White Christmas" treats and, because it's summer, a cool glass of milk or beer. Boys and girls who are too excited to sleep might hear the sound of the bell Santa rings as he leaves their home.

JAPAN

In Japan, Hoteiosha brings gifts and fortunes to children. They believe he has eyes in the back of his head so he can watch for children who are misbehaving. After he leaves their gifts on their pillow, Hoteiosha enjoys a slice of strawberry-topped Christmas cake the children put out for him.

INDONESIA

Most homes in Indonesia don't have chimneys, so children put their shoes near the door or in front of a pretend fireplace they make for Sinterklaas to fill with gifts. In return, children treat him to a taste of the tropics with *nastar* cookies filled with pineapple jam.

PHILIPPINES

Before they go to bed, Filipino children double-check to make sure their parents leave the front door unlatched for Santa Claus to come in. After filling the stockings, Santa finds the children's gift of *puto seko,* a crisp, melt-in-your-mouth cookie, and a spicy ginger tea called *salabat.*

SRI LANKA

On Christmas Eve in Sri Lanka, children come home from midnight mass and hang their stockings on the tree. After Naththal Seeya (Christmas Grandfather) puts their gifts in the stockings, he munches on *kokis*, a lacey fried cookie, while he sips the Ceylon tea the island country is famous for.

INDIA

Children in India hang their stockings by a window if they don't have a fireplace. They leave Christmas Baba (Father Christmas) a crispy fried treat called *kulkuls* and a cup of spicy chai.

SOUTH AFRICA

Kersvader (Father Christmas) arrives in South Africa by donkey. He fills children's stockings with special chocolates and small gifts. They leave him *hertzog* cookies, filled with apricot jam and topped with crunchy coconut meringue.

MALAWI

In Malawi, Father Christmas brings gifts to children at Christmas parties at their school. They thank him with *mbatata* (sweet potato cookies).

BETHLEHEM

As the site of the first Christmas, many people from around the world visit Bethlehem for this special holiday. Santa brings gifts to children in homes with a cross painted over the door. Children give him *ma'moul,* a cookie stuffed with dates or honey and nuts.

EGYPT

Children in Egypt go to bed early in hopes that Baba Noel will climb through the window, enjoy the *kahk* (a sweet biscuit) they put out for him, and leave them gifts.

RUSSIA

In Russia, Ded Moroz (Grandfather Frost) brings
Snegurochka (Snow Maiden) to deliver gifts. She
rides in a sleigh pulled by three horses. Children
give them a gift of *pryaniki*, a sweet honey-spice
cookie, and a cup of tea to warm them for the
rest of their journey.

UKRAINE

Svyatyy Mykolay (Saint Nickolas) slips in quietly to put gifts under the pillow of children in Ukraine. They leave a traditional Saint Nick cookie, *mykolaichiki*, for him.

DENMARK

In Denmark, Julemande (Christmas Man) puts presents under the tree while the family eats Christmas dinner. When everyone is finished eating, the children see the decorated tree for the first time. They thank Julemande in person for their gifts by sharing their *risalamande* (rice pudding) with him.

NORWAY

Nearby in Norway, Julenissen (Christmas Elf) comes into the house on Christmas Eve and asks, "Are there any good children here?" Sometimes the children must sing for him before they receive their gifts. Julenissen is thanked with some *riskrem*—a sweet rice pudding served with a cherry sauce.

POLAND

The Star Man visits families in Poland after their Christmas dinner. He asks the children questions and rewards their answers with small gifts. In return, they share fruit-filled *kolaczki* with him and his companions, the Star Boys, who sing for the family.

GERMANY

German children have been counting down the days until Christmas on their advent calendars. They open the last door on the advent calendar before they go to bed, excited to see what they will find under the tree from Weihnachtsmann (Christmas Man). Making many kinds of Christmas cookies is an important part of Christmas celebrations in Germany. Children leave Weihnachtsmann a plate filled with *Pepparkkakor, Springerle,* and gingerbread people.

FRANCE

In France, children leave carrots, oats, or apples in the shoes they place by the fireplace or Christmas tree. Père Noël takes the children's gifts to Gui, the donkey who carries his heavy sack. Then he fills the shoes with small gifts and treats (sometimes they borrow shoes from their parents because they hold more). For himself, Père Noël can choose from any of the thirteen desserts families eat during their Christmas Eve celebration. He really likes to have a slice of the yule log with the glass of wine they leave for him.

SPAIN

Spanish children fall into bed late, tired from their festive Noche Buena celebration that brings many family and friends together for a big meal and singing and dancing.

They put their shoes on their windowsill or balcony filled with treats of barley and wheat for the Wise Men's horses. One of the Wise Men leaves the children gifts. *Turrón,* a nougat candy of almonds, honey, and sugar, is the most popular Christmas treat to leave as a gift.

In the Basque Country that lies between France and Spain, Olentzero, a coal miner from the Pyrenees Mountains, brings coal for the bad children and gifts for the good. Children clean their shoes and place them near the fireplace for him to fill. Children thank Olentzero for their gifts by leaving a glass of wine and almond tile cookies, which are shaped like the roof tiles on their homes.

GREAT BRITAIN

Father Christmas fills the stockings of children in Great Britain. They leave him a gift of fruit-filled mince pie along with a glass of sherry.

IRELAND

Santa must be very quiet as he slips in to fill the stockings hung at the foot of the bed in Irish homes. Like in Great Britain, he'll find a mince pie and glass of milk (and sometimes Guinness) on the table, along with a candle that will burn all night.

BRAZIL

When he visits Brazil, Papai Noel comes in the front door and finds the children's shoes beside the Christmas tree or *prescepio* (Nativity scene) or next to their beds, waiting to be filled with gifts. Children leave him a fudgelike sweet called *brigadeiro*.

ARGENTINA

In Argentina, Papa Noel has to wait until the big fireworks displays are over before the children will be asleep for his visit. Boys and girls fill their shoes with straw or barley for his camels, and leave Papa Noel *mantecados de anis*, a crumbly cookie with a hint of licorice flavor, and *sidra*, a sparkling cider.

CHILE

Chimneys in Chile are too narrow for Viejo Pascuero (Old Man Christmas), so he climbs in a window. He leaves presents near the manger scene and finds a plate with a gift of *pan de pascqua*, a Christmas bread filled with candied fruit.

PUERTO RICO

Boys and girls in Puerto Rico leave straw in shoeboxes under their beds for the camels of the Wise Men. They also leave *mantecadito,* a cherry-studded shortbread cookie for the Wise Men, who bring the children gifts.

COSTA RICA

Colacho brings gifts to children in Costa Rica and puts them under the fragrant cypress tree. Costa Rican children leave him a gift of crunchy, star-shaped *suspiros* and a glass of *rompope*—eggnog flavored with coconut.

MEXICO

Just after midnight, Mexican children get to break open a piñata filled with small toys and treats. After they go to bed, Santa arrives to bring their gifts. He looks forward to the nutty, sugar-coated Mexican wedding cookies they leave for him, along with a cup of sweet, spicy Mexican hot chocolate that warms him up as he heads further north again, where it's cold.

UNITED STATES

All across America, children have decorated their trees and hung their stockings, waiting for Santa and his reindeer to arrive. From Maine to California, and all the states in between, Santa will find a glass of milk and a plate of cookies. Children might choose to give him decorated gingerbread people, iced sugar cookies, or the classic American chocolate chip cookie. They also sometimes leave carrots for Santa's reindeer.

CANADA

The nights are long in the northernmost part of North America, but Santa Claus finds his way to Montreal, Canada, by the millions of Christmas lights on display across the city—they can be seen from space! In the French-speaking region of Quebec, Père Noël warms himself by the fire while he fills children's stockings and enjoys the spicy, fruit-filled hermit cookies they leave. They're perfect for dunking in the milk the children leave with the cookies.

As he gets to Canada's western coast, Father Christmas appreciates the warm pot of tea and rich, layered Nanaimo bars the children leave for him.

ALASKA

When Santa arrives in Alaska, he's pretty close to his North Pole home (there is a town called North Pole, Alaska, but that's different). Alaskan children give him Eskimo cookies: a chewy, fudgy oatmeal cookie that is cooked on top of the stove, not in the oven.

HAWAII

Hawaiian children won't hear the sound of hoofs on their roofs, but they might see Santa's footprints in the sand where he hopped off the surfboard pulled by a dolphin. Kanakaloka comes through the windows that are left open to allow the cooling trade winds to blow through. Children will find their gifts under the trees they decorate with garlands, shells, and starfish. The present they give him of sweet, chewy pineapple-macadamia bars is a refreshing treat.

After visiting the last home in Pago-Pago, Santa flies back to the wintry North Pole. He's warmed by the thoughts of the joy the boys and girls he visited will feel as they open their gifts, and by sweet memories of the giving spirit children everywhere showed through the treats they shared with him.

Turn the page to see recipes for many of the holiday treats mentioned in this story. Maybe you'll find something new to leave Santa this year!

AUTHOR'S NOTE

In *A World of Cookies for Santa*, we looked at one tasty aspect of Christmas traditions around the world. Countries celebrate differently, but they all have in common the tradition of preparing and enjoying treats from their culture—many of which come from recipes that go back for generations.

In some countries, Christmas celebrations begin far earlier than December 24 and continue well after December 25. For example, Saint Nicholas Day (December 6) is observed in many countries as the day Saint Nick brings presents to children.

Many countries observe Epiphany on January 6. Children in these countries often get presents from "the Three Kings"—in fact, the observance is often called Three Kings Day in addition to Epiphany.

Some countries have a unique gift-bringer in addition to their version of Santa Claus. Some examples are . . .

- Italy's La Befana is an old woman said to have turned away the Three Kings on their way to see the baby Jesus. After she realized her mistake, she filled a bag with gifts for the baby Jesus, but didn't find him. Now she travels in search of the Christ Child, and gives gifts to other children along the way.

- In Germany, Christkind is like an angel who delivers gifts.

- France's Le Père Fouettard is said to travel with Père Noël to punish naughty children while good children receive their gifts.

I hope this taste of traditions and treats from around the world will be just the beginning of your exploration of how children around the world celebrate this special holiday. If you're interested in learning more, visit our website at **www.worldofcookiesforsanta.com** where we'll be sharing more cookies and customs and invite you to share yours with us.

Have a delicious Christmas!

RECIPES

Christmas Island—COCONUT MACAROONS

Sweetened condensed milk is a favorite ingredient on Christmas Island, as it's easier to store than fresh milk. Combined with coconut, it makes a sweet, moist cookie.

Ingredients

1 14-oz package flaked coconut

¼ cup flour

1 14-oz can sweetened condensed milk

2 teaspoons vanilla or almond extract

Directions

1. Preheat oven to 325 degrees F (160 degrees C). Grease baking sheets, or line with baking parchment.

2. In a large mixing bowl, combine coconut and flour.

3. In another bowl, stir together sweetened condensed milk and vanilla or almond extract.

4. Pour sweetened condensed milk mixture into coconut and flour, stirring until well mixed.

5. Using an ice cream scoop or ⅛ cup measuring cup, scoop mixture and press lightly to pack well.

6. Drop onto parchment-lined or well-greased baking sheets.

7. Bake 12 to 15 minutes or until lightly browned around the edges.

8. Immediately remove from baking sheets and cool on racks. Store loosely covered at room temperature. Makes about 18 cookies.

New Zealand—ANZAC BISCUITS

These sweet, crisp cookies were created to ship to troops from Australia and New Zealand. They ship and keep well in tins.

Ingredients

1 cup quick cooking oats

1 cup all-purpose flour

1 cup white sugar

¾ cup flaked coconut

½ cup butter

1 tablespoon golden syrup*

2 tablespoons boiling water

1 teaspoon baking soda

Directions

1. Preheat oven to 350 degrees F (175 degrees C). Grease cookie sheets or line with parchment paper.

2. In a large bowl, combine oats, flour, sugar, and coconut; set aside.

3. In a small saucepan over low heat, melt the butter and syrup together.

4. Add the soda to the boiling water and pour into the melted butter and syrup.

5. Add butter mixture to the dry ingredients. Stir until well blended.

6. Drop by teaspoons onto prepared cookie sheets.

7. Bake for 18 to 20 minutes, until golden and slightly firm.

8. Cool briefly on pans, then move to wire rack and cool completely. Keeps well in airtight container. Makes about 2 dozen cookies.

*Sometimes found in specialty stores, especially those with foods imported from England. If you can't find golden syrup, you can substitute light corn syrup.

Philippine Islands—PUTO SEKO

This light, crisp cookie uses cornstarch instead of flour, which makes it melt in your mouth. (And it's gluten free!)

Ingredients

1 cup butter, softened

1 cup sugar

3 eggs

3 ⅔ cups cornstarch

1 teaspoon cream of tartar

1 teaspoon baking powder

Directions

1. Preheat the oven to 375 degrees F (190 degrees C). Grease cookie sheets.

2. In a medium bowl, cream together the butter and sugar until light and smooth.

3. Beat in the eggs, one at a time.

4. Add cornstarch, cream of tartar, and baking powder, stirring until well blended.

5. Roll the dough into 1-inch balls and place them 1 inch apart on the prepared cookie sheets.

6. Bake for 10 to 12 minutes in the preheated oven, or until light brown.

7. Remove to wire racks to cool. Makes about 3 dozen cookies.

Basque Country—ALMOND TILE COOKIES

Ingredients

2 egg whites

½ cup superfine sugar

⅛ teaspoon salt

½ teaspoon almond extract

¼ teaspoon vanilla extract

1 tablespoon butter, melted

¼ cup cake flour

¼ cup sliced almonds

Directions

1. Preheat oven to 400 degrees F (200 degrees C). Generously grease two baking sheets (or line with parchment paper).

2. In a medium bowl, beat egg whites, sugar, salt, extracts, and butter on low speed until foamy.

3. Sift in cake flour and gently fold into mixture.

4. Drop tablespoonfuls of batter about four inches apart onto greased cookie sheets (about two per sheet). Use spatula to spread dough into very thin circles, about 3 inches each.

5. Sprinkle with a few sliced almonds.

6. Bake, one cookie sheet at a time, for 6 to 8 minutes or until edges are just browned and centers are golden.

7. Using a thin spatula, quickly remove from one sheet at a time and drape cookie over rolling pin to shape. Allow to cool completely on rolling pin.

8. Repeat steps 4 through 7 with rest of batter. Work with only two to four cookies at a time so you have time to shape them. (If cookies get too crisp to work with, return to oven for no more than one additional minute.)

9. To retain crispness, store cool cookies in a single layer in an airtight container. Makes 2½ dozen cookies.

Puerto Rico—MANTECADITOS

Ingredients

2¼ cups all-purpose flour

¼ teaspoon freshly ground nutmeg

¾ cup butter, softened

¼ cup vegetable shortening

1½ teaspoons almond extract

½ teaspoon vanilla extract

½ cup sugar

5 maraschino cherries, each cut into eight pieces

Directions

1. Place oven rack in middle position of the oven. Preheat oven to 350 F (175 degrees C).

2. Combine flour and nutmeg; set aside.

3. In a large mixing bowl, beat butter, shortening, and extracts with an electric mixer on medium-high speed until smooth.

4. Gradually add sugar to butter mixture and mix together until light and fluffy.

5. Blend in flour mixture a little at a time. Dough should be slightly moist. If dough looks dry, sprinkle with water and work into dough. If dough is sticky, sprinkle with additional flour.

6. Spoon dough by teaspoons and form into balls. Place on an ungreased baking sheet. Gently press each ball with palm of hand to form cookie. Garnish with a cherry piece pressed into the center of each cookie.

7. Bake 20 minutes or until golden.

8. Remove to a wire rack to cool. Makes about 40 cookies.

Mexico—MEXICAN WEDDING COOKIES

Many countries have a version of this crumbly, nutty cookie. In Russia, they're Russian teacakes, in Spain, *polvorones*, in Greece, *kourabiedes*. My grandmother called them snowballs. This might be the most universal of all cookies.

Ingredients

1 cup butter, softened

1 teaspoon vanilla extract

6 tablespoons confectioners' sugar

2 cups all-purpose flour

1 cup chopped walnuts

⅓ cup confectioners' sugar for decoration

Directions

1. Preheat oven to 350 degrees F (175 degrees C).

2. In a medium bowl, cream butter and vanilla until smooth.

3. Combine the 6 tablespoons confectioners' sugar and flour; stir into the butter mixture until just blended.

4. Mix in the chopped walnuts.

5. Roll dough into 1-inch balls and place them 2 inches apart on an ungreased cookie sheet.

6. Bake for 12 minutes. Roll in remaining confectioners' sugar while still warm. Roll them in powdered sugar a second time when cool. Makes 3 dozen cookies.

Canada—HERMIT COOKIES

Hermits are chewy when they come out of the oven but crisp once they cool, perfect for dipping in milk.

Ingredients

½ cup (1 stick) butter or margarine, softened

¾ cup packed brown sugar

1 egg

2 tablespoons milk

1 teaspoon vanilla extract

1½ cups flour

½ teaspoon baking soda

½ teaspoon ground cinnamon

¼ teaspoon ground nutmeg

⅛ teaspoon ground cloves

1 cup raisins or mixed, diced dried fruit

½ cup chopped walnuts or almonds

Directions

1. Preheat oven to 375 degrees F (190 degrees C); lightly grease baking sheets.

2. In a large mixing bowl, beat together butter and brown sugar until fluffy.

3. Beat in egg and milk, add vanilla extract and mix.

4. Add flour, baking soda, cinnamon, nutmeg, and cloves. Mix until thoroughly combined.

5. Stir in raisins or mixed fruit and nuts.

6. Drop by teaspoonfuls onto prepared baking sheets.

7. Bake 8 to 10 minutes or until edges are lightly browned.

8. Cool on a wire rack and store in an airtight container. Makes 3 dozen cookies.

Alaska—ESKIMO COOKIES

Eskimo cookies are sometimes called "no-bakes." These fudgey cookies are very easy to make and are almost more candy than cookie.

Ingredients

½ cup butter

2 cups sugar

6 tablespoons cocoa

½ cup milk

3 cups oats (regular or quick cook but not instant)

1 teaspoon vanilla

½ teaspoon salt

Directions

1. In medium saucepan, heat butter, milk, sugar, and cocoa over medium heat until sugar is dissolved, stirring constantly (about 5 minutes).

2. Once it comes to a full boil, boil for one minute, stirring constantly.

3. Remove from heat and cool mixture in pan for 5 minutes.

4. Stir in oatmeal, vanilla, and salt.

5. Drop by teaspoonfuls onto waxed paper or foil and allow to cool completely.

6. Store in an airtight container. Makes about 4 dozen cookies.

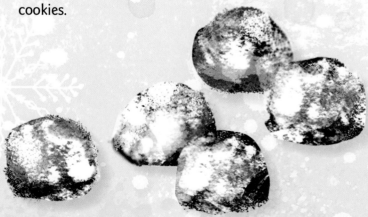

Hawaii—PINEAPPLE MACADAMIA BARS

These sweet cookie bars have some of the flavors Hawaii is most famous for—coconut, pineapple, and macadamia nuts.

Ingredients

Crust:

½ cup butter, room temperature

¼ cup light brown sugar, packed

1 cup sifted all-purpose flour

Filling:

¼ cup sifted all-purpose flour

½ teaspoon baking powder

¼ teaspoon salt

2 eggs, beaten

1 cup light brown sugar, packed

1 cup flaked coconut

¼ cup well-drained crushed pineapple

¾ cup toasted chopped macadamia nuts, almonds, or pecans*

Directions

Crust

1. Preheat oven to 350 degrees F (175 degrees C). Grease 9-inch square pan.

2. In small bowl, stir together butter, brown sugar, and flour. Combine until blended.

3. Spread evenly on prepared pan, pressing lightly.

4. Bake crust for 10 minutes, until just starting to brown. Remove from oven and set aside.

Filling:

1. In a small bowl, sift together flour, baking powder, and salt.

2. In large mixing bowl, beat together eggs and brown sugar.

3. Stir flour mixture into eggs and brown sugar.

4. Add coconut, pineapple, and nuts. Stir to combine well.

5. Spread topping mixture evenly over baked crust.

6. Bake 25 to 30 minutes until golden around edges and set.

7. Cool for about 10 minutes, then cut into bars and allow to cool completely. Makes about 12 bars.

*To toast nuts, spread out in a single layer in an ungreased skillet over medium heat, stirring, until golden brown.

10

31
ALASKA

23

7

3

30
CANADA

32
HAWAII

31

28

32

29
UNITED STATES

28
MEXICO

26
PUERTO
RICO

27
COSTA
RICA

23
BRAZIL

25
CHILE

24
ARGENTINA

11

4

13

12

8

9

20

21 & 22

14

17